Tyndale House Publishers, Inc., Carol Stream, Illinois

So Long,
Insecurity

devotional journal

BETH MOORE

Visit Tyndale's exciting website at www.tyndale.com.

Visit Living Proof's website at www.LProof.org.

TYNDALE and Tyndale's quill logo are registered trademarks of Tyndale House Publishers, Inc.

So Long, Insecurity Devotional Journal

Designed by Jacqueline L. Nuñez

Published in association with Yates & Yates (www.yates2.com).

ISBN 978-1-4143-4992-3

Printed in the United States of America

17   16   15   14   13   12   11
7   6   5   4   3   2   1

Introduction

This is the confidence we have in approaching God:
that if we ask anything according to his will, he hears us.
And if we know that he hears us—whatever we ask—
we know that we have what we asked of him.

1 JOHN 5:14–15

Insecurity can be crushing. It can paralyze you and mock you and make you feel completely unworthy of ever fully grasping any of the great gifts God wants to give you—even those He has already given.

You know exactly what I'm talking about. Surely you hear the same echoes of fear and desperation that I do—women trying to measure up to the airbrushed images on every magazine cover, women giving away their bodies in hopes of holding on to their men, women trying to do all and have all and be all.

Something is wrong with us that we value ourselves so little. Especially when God values us so very much. If you've read *So Long, Insecurity* or participated in the *So Long, Insecurity Group Experience,* you know that my determined goal and lofty hope is that every woman will find herself being loosed from the grip of insecurity. We desperately need to get our dignity back, but if we only talk about it, we'll find ourselves better informed but no less insecure. I'd like you to join me on a personal quest for authentic, soul-deep security.

That quest begins with a supernatural act of God Himself, as He allows you to draw from the bottomless sea of His divine strength. Hear this at a yell: it is God's will for you to have your dignity and security restored. You don't need to wrestle with this one. You don't need to read six more books. You don't need to ponder the subject matter until your next big disaster. This one is cut and dried. There are plenty of times when the precise will of God on a matter seems legitimately unclear—you may not know whether He's leading you to change jobs, marry a certain guy, or relocate, for instance. But after twenty-five years of study, I can promise you this: God's will is for us to walk out the depth and breadth of our lives with dignity and security. Neither God nor you have anything to gain by your persistent insecurity.

When it comes to dignity and security, we have a golden opportunity to know in advance that we are praying the will of God for our lives. And we need to cash in on that request posthaste. We can count on the answer being as sure as the appeal. In fact, if you're willing to exercise the kind of boldness that excites the heart of God, you can go right ahead and thank Him in advance, because you know that what you've asked is as good as done. Sometimes we see or sense the evidence immediately. Other times God lets it amass bit by bit.

In this devotional journal, we'll tackle the problem of insecurity one day at a time, one issue at a time. As we go, I encourage you to use this book to document your journey: the challenges you face, the prayers you pray, the victories you experience along the way. As you do, you'll be creating a record that you can look back upon for years to come—an account of the ways God has helped you reclaim your dignity and prime your soul for security.

So here's what I'm asking you to do. Set aside some time and find a private place where you can be undisturbed and undistracted. If you can take a little longer to process the meditations, the healing and transformation will be more substantial. Some of you may even have the means to get away overnight and have a retreat of sorts with God. That would be fantastic, but don't let logistical arrangements keep you from accomplishing the goal. Better to take that half an hour now and get it done! Whatever block of time you set aside, make a determined choice to put everything else on hold for that segment. Rest assured, what you are doing alone with God during those moments will also benefit every other relationship and circumstance in your life. Set all other priorities aside for a while so that a healthier soul can pick them back up again.

Find a comfortable spot where you can come before God— someplace where you can sit, kneel, or even lie facedown. Some of those postures might be new for you, but don't get antsy. We're not being all mystical here. We're simply being mindful. You can find examples throughout Scripture where people take on postures of prayer that reflect their sincerity. No matter what position you choose, you can count on the absolute certainty that God will hear you and meet with you through the power of His Spirit.

Once you've determined your time, place, and posture, you can begin working through the journal pages that follow. Read each question and passage slowly, thoughtfully, and even out loud, if you find that helpful. Ask God to equip you with His supernatural wisdom and insight, and then trust that He will answer your earnest request.

As a concept resonates, document it on the pages of this journal and then spend some time in prayer. Pray with honesty from the depths of your heart to God. If you use the prayer guides, the only thing I ask is that you make the petitions your own by truly *meaning* them. When I word something that is different from how you feel or what you've experienced, rephrase that portion with your own words and record your prayer in the space provided. Documenting and personalizing this experience will be the lifeblood of your journey. You will be able to reflect on this process for years to come and remember where your road to security began. You will also be able to return to this journal and pray through it when insecurity sneaks up on you again—and invariably it will.

That said, pray on, dear one. And let God have complete access to your soul as you do.

Love,
  Beth

Section 1

Blessed are those who trust in the LORD
and have made the LORD their hope and confidence.
They are like trees planted along a riverbank,
with roots that reach deep into the water.
Such trees are not bothered by the heat
or worried by long months of drought.
Their leaves stay green,
and they never stop producing fruit.

JEREMIAH 17:7–8, NLT

Insecurity: A Bad Friend

In one way or another, insecurity has made fools of all of us. Naturally, we'd just as soon not remember how. But, dear one, if we're going to get serious about letting God deliver us, we must look in the mirror and realize how far we are from God's original intent for us. Until we do that, we'll continue to settle for what we have.

Being set free from something as innate as chronic insecurity will take a little time. But God promises to help us see where we're broken—and why. We can start the healing process *today* as we begin recognizing triggers and responding to them differently. Even though we may still *feel* insecure, we can make a deliberate choice to not act on that feeling.

In what areas of your own life do you feel the most insecure?

_____

_____

_____

_____

_____

_____

_____

_____

_____

_____

_____

_____

_____

_____

_____

_____

_____

_____

_____

_____

_____

The enemy pursues me,
he crushes me to the ground;
he makes me dwell in the darkness
like those long dead.

PSALM 143:3

Insecurity is truly a bad friend—even an enemy—to all of us.
How has keeping company with such a "friend" damaged you
spiritually, emotionally, mentally, or physically?

_____

_____

_____

_____

_____

_____

_____

_____

_____

_____

_____

_____

_____

_____

_____

_____

_____

_____

I cling to you;
your strong right hand holds me securely.

PSALM 63:8, NLT

Society encourages us to find our security in many things other than God: money, beauty, work, sexuality, relationships, certain roles, etc. What things have you put your trust in that eventually let you down?

_____

_____

_____

_____

_____

_____

_____

_____

_____

_____

_____

_____

_____

_____

_____

_____

*Don't copy the behavior and customs of this world, but
let God transform you into a new person by changing the
way you think. Then you will learn to know God's will
for you, which is good and pleasing and perfect.*

ROMANS 12:2, NLT

In what areas of your life do you desperately need to put your hope and confidence in the Lord? What changes do you sense He wants to make in you?

_____

_____

_____

_____

_____

_____

_____

_____

_____

_____

_____

_____

_____

_____

_____

_____

_____

_____

_____

_____

From everlasting to everlasting
the LORD's love is with those who fear him,
and his righteousness with their children's children—
with those who keep his covenant
and remember to obey his precepts.

PSALM 103:17–18

The Lord created you and loves you. How do you think He feels about your struggle with insecurity?

_____

_____

_____

_____

_____

_____

_____

_____

_____

_____

_____

_____

_____

_____

_____

_____

_____

_____

_____

_____

As a father has compassion on his children,
so the LORD has compassion on those who fear him;
for he knows how we are formed,
he remembers that we are dust.

PSALM 103:13–14

What are the characteristics of a truly secure person? How would your thoughts, feelings, and actions be different if you were rooted more firmly in the Lord?

_____

_____

_____

_____

_____

_____

_____

_____

_____

_____

_____

_____

_____

_____

_____

_____

_____

_____

_____

_____

_____

_____

Those who trust in the LORD are as secure as Mount Zion;
they will not be defeated but will endure forever.
Just as the mountains surround Jerusalem,
so the LORD surrounds his people, both now and forever.

PSALM 125:1-2, NLT

Dear God,

I come to You this moment because I need some things only You can give me. I need restoration, Lord. I need my dignity back. You alone know what insecurity has cost me, what trouble—even torment—it has caused me. You are intimately acquainted with every time it's made a fool of me. You know how hard I've fought to play the game, but You also know that in the aftermath I've been defeated. I'm sick of faking. I'm sick of sulking. I desperately need and want to be delivered from my chronic insecurity. I am ready to discover what it means to be truly secure. I am willing to do whatever it takes to be free and to allow You to do through me what I cannot do for myself. You are the all-powerful, all-knowing Maker of heaven and earth and the grand Weaver of every human soul. You alone know how we are made and who we're meant to be. I'm not asking for anything You're not willing to give me. You have not shortchanged me. I have shortchanged myself and allowed my culture to sell me short.

You know the way I'm formed. You know what motivates me. You know what shuts me down. You know how driven I am by fear and how exhausted I am from surrendering to it. Lord, in the most hidden places, I am so afraid that . . .

_____

_____

_____

_____

_____

_____

_____

_____

_____

_____

_____

_____

_____

_____

_____

_____

_____

_____

_____

_____

_____

_____

Section 2

How precious are your thoughts about me, O God.
They cannot be numbered!

PSALM 139:17, NLT

The Effects of Insecurity

Although we may have something unhealthy deep inside of us, those in whom Christ dwells also have something deeper. Something whole. Something so infinitely healthy that, if it would but invade the rest of us, we would be healed.

I am so thankful that at no time since I received Christ as Savior have I ever been a total wreck. Partial? Lord, have mercy, yes. Humiliatingly so.

But total? Not on your ever-loving life. And if He resides in you, neither have you.

Insecurity is often defined as "self-sabotage." As you think about its effects in your own life, how would you describe it?

_____

_____

_____

_____

_____

_____

_____

_____

_____

_____

_____

_____

_____

_____

_____

_____

_____

We are hard pressed on every side, but not crushed;
perplexed, but not in despair; persecuted, but not
abandoned; struck down, but not destroyed.

2 CORINTHIANS 4:8-9

In what areas of your life does insecurity keep you from using your gifts or doing the things you want to do?

_____

_____

_____

_____

_____

_____

_____

_____

_____

_____

_____

_____

_____

_____

_____

_____

_____

_____

*There is no fear in love. But perfect love drives out
fear, because fear has to do with punishment. The
one who fears is not made perfect in love.*

1 JOHN 4:18

In what ways has insecurity caused you to place unrealistic expectations on the relationships in your life?

_____

_____

_____

_____

_____

_____

_____

_____

_____

_____

_____

_____

_____

_____

_____

_____

_____

Whom have I in heaven but you?
I desire you more than anything on earth.

PSALM 73:25, NLT

We all have false positives in our lives—the one or two things we think would make us more secure. What are yours?

_____

_____

_____

_____

_____

_____

_____

_____

_____

_____

_____

_____

_____

_____

_____

_____

_____

_____

Don't store up treasures here on earth, where moths eat them and rust destroys them, and where thieves break in and steal. Store your treasures in heaven. . . . Wherever your treasure is, there the desires of your heart will also be.

MATTHEW 6:19-21, NLT

If God were to write a description of you, what would He say?

_____

_____

_____

_____

_____

_____

_____

_____

_____

_____

_____

_____

_____

_____

_____

_____

_____

_____

_____

_____

_____

*O LORD, you have examined my heart
and know everything about me.*

PSALM 139:1, NLT

God formed you in your mother's womb, and He knows everything about you. What does this tell you about the way He
views you?

_____

_____

_____

_____

_____

_____

_____

_____

_____

_____

_____

_____

_____

_____

_____

_____

_____

_____

_____

_____

_____

_____

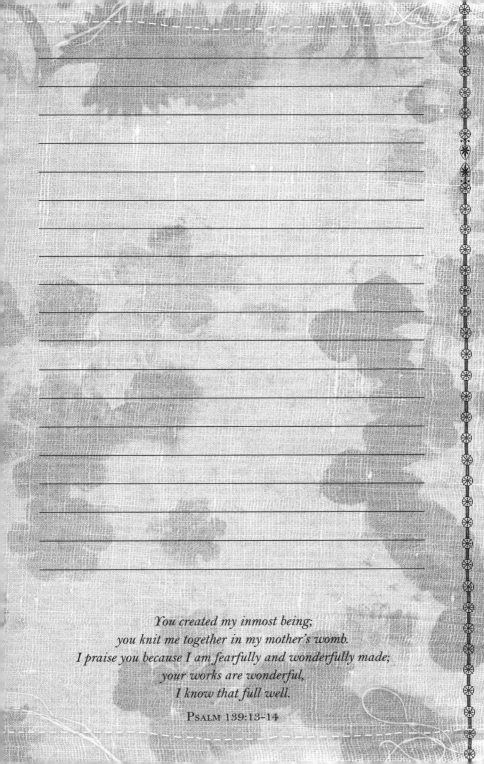

You created my inmost being;
you knit me together in my mother's womb.
I praise you because I am fearfully and wonderfully made;
your works are wonderful,
I know that full well.

PSALM 139:13–14

The Bible says God considers you His "masterpiece." How does this affect the way you perceive yourself?

_____

_____

_____

_____

_____

_____

_____

_____

_____

_____

_____

_____

_____

_____

_____

_____

We are God's masterpiece. He has created us anew in Christ Jesus, so we can do the good things he planned for us long ago.

EPHESIANS 2:10, NLT

Consider the way God made you—your physical and psychological makeup, your skills and abilities, your gifts and talents. What do these characteristics tell you about some of the purposes He might have for your life?

_____

_____

_____

_____

_____

_____

_____

_____

_____

_____

_____

_____

_____

_____

_____

_____

_____

_____

God has given each of you a gift from his great variety
of spiritual gifts. Use them well to serve one another.

1 PETER 4:10, NLT

Dear God,

Deliver me, Lord. You have not given me a spirit of fear but of power, love, and a sound mind. That's what Scripture says. I claim each of those priceless traits as mine this day. Your desire is for me to be free of every unhealthy motivation. Reveal any place they reside uncontested in me, and supply the courage I need to refuse to do their bidding. You have searched the deepest recesses of my heart and mind. I don't need to hide anything from You or act stronger or more together than I am. Help me to come before You with complete transparency, and grant me a supernatural confidence that I am safe with You and loved by You. I don't have to muster feelings I don't possess or hang my head in defeat and shame. Because of Your grace, I can come to You just as I am. This is the way I would describe myself to You right now:

_____

_____

_____

_____

_____

Section 3

I sought the LORD, and he answered me;
he delivered me from all my fears.

PSALM 34:4

Good Company

The fact that the inspiration of the Holy Spirit on the pages of Scripture is not dampened by the insecurities of those God chose to pen it is perhaps the greatest testimony to its incomparable potency. After reading about the likes of Adam, Eve, Abraham, Sarah, Hagar, Leah, Rachel, Saul, the woman at the well, the "super-apostles," and Paul, surely we can breathe a sigh of relief that we are not alone in our struggles.

Human flesh and blood have no weakness so strong that God's strength is made weak. He's got what we need. It's up to us whether we're going to let the worst of us get the best of us.

Insecurity is often rooted in fear. What or whom are you most afraid of?

_____

_____

_____

_____

_____

_____

_____

_____

_____

_____

_____

_____

_____

_____

_____

_____

_____

_____

God has not given us a spirit of fear and timidity,
but of power, love, and self-discipline.

2 TIMOTHY 1:7, NLT

Which biblical character or characters do you most closely relate to? Why?

_____

_____

_____

_____

_____

_____

_____

_____

_____

_____

_____

_____

_____

_____

_____

_____

_____

All these people earned a good reputation because of their faith, yet none of them received all that God had promised.

HEBREWS 11:39, NLT

Make a list of the insecurities your favorite Bible characters may have had to deal with.

_____

_____

_____

_____

_____

_____

_____

_____

_____

_____

_____

_____

_____

_____

_____

_____

_____

By faith these people overthrew kingdoms, ruled with
justice, and received what God had promised them.
. . . Their weakness was turned to strength.

HEBREWS 11:33-34, NLT

How do you react to valid threats or fears? When they prompt intense feelings of insecurity, what tools could you use to deal with them?

_____

_____

_____

_____

_____

_____

_____

_____

_____

_____

_____

_____

_____

_____

_____

You are my hiding place;
you will protect me from trouble
and surround me with songs of deliverance.

PSALM 32:7

When have you been guilty of the "imposter syndrome"—
pretending to be someone or something you are not?

_____

_____

_____

_____

_____

_____

_____

_____

_____

_____

_____

_____

_____

_____

He reveals the deep things of darkness
and brings utter darkness into the light.

JOB 12:22

Insecurity is often tied to loss. What or whom do you most fear losing? How does that fuel your insecurities?

_____

_____

_____

_____

_____

_____

_____

_____

_____

_____

_____

_____

_____

_____

_____

_____

_____

I consider everything a loss because of the surpassing worth of knowing Christ Jesus my Lord, for whose sake I have lost all things. I consider them garbage, that I may gain Christ.

PHILIPPIANS 3:8

What are some of the weaknesses or "thorns in the flesh" in your life? What would it look like to surrender those areas to the Lord?

_____

_____

_____

_____

_____

_____

_____

_____

_____

_____

_____

_____

_____

_____

_____

_____

_____

_____

_____

_To keep me from becoming proud, I was given a thorn in
my flesh, a messenger from Satan to torment me and keep
me from becoming proud. Three different times I begged
the Lord to take it away. Each time he said, "My grace
is all you need. My power works best in weakness."_

2 CORINTHIANS 12:7–9, NLT

In what ways have you experienced the sufficiency of God's grace? Where do you need it most today?

_____

_____

_____

_____

_____

_____

_____

_____

_____

_____

_____

_____

_____

_____

_____

_____

He will be the sure foundation for your times,
a rich store of salvation and wisdom and knowledge;
the fear of the LORD is the key to this treasure.

ISAIAH 33:6

Dear Lord,

I now ask You to single out everything You entrusted to me as part of my physical and psychological makeup: personal limitations, my appearance, and my God-given disposition. You knew what You were doing when You formed me in my mother's womb. Nothing is without purpose. Nothing has thrown off the plan. Every gift, challenge, and obstacle is meant to shape the specific destiny You ordained for me before time began. Your intent is to make a wonder out of me and show what You can do through me. You mean to increase the praise that comes to You because of my life. You want to defy the odds in order to make Yourself conspicuous in me. Please deliver me from self-pity and a life of excuses and rationalizations. And Lord, where I've otherwise lapsed into self-adoration and self-centeredness instead, help me to recognize my narcissism and no longer tolerate it. Of all things, please don't let it be said that I loved myself too much to fully love anybody else. Please don't let me gain the world but lose my soul.

Lord, even in the midst of all these requests,

I thank You with my whole heart for working so diligently in my life. Yes, there have been people who have hurt me and have done a very poor job of taking Your place, but there have also been people who have shown me glimpses of You. Not perfect people, but genuine people. In particular, I thank You for . . .

_____

_____

_____

_____

_____

_____

_____

_____

_____

_____

_____

_____

_____

_____

_____

_____

_____

Section 4

Christ will make his home in your hearts as you trust in him.
Your roots will grow down into God's love and keep you strong.

EPHESIANS 3:17, NLT

The Roots of Insecurity

I hate to display such a firm grasp of the obvious, but how will we ever change if everything around us stays the same? Or what will ever cause us to move on to the next place He has for us if something doesn't happen to change the way we feel about where we are? God is thoroughly committed to finishing the masterpiece He started in us. And that process means one major thing: change.

Which of the following roots of insecurity do you relate to the most?

Instability in the home (abuse, divorce, illness, financial difficulties)

Significant loss

Rejection

Dramatic change

Personal limitations

Personal disposition and temperament

Our culture and the pressure it puts on women to be young and beautiful

Pride

_____

_____

_____

_____

_____

_____

_____

_____

_____

_____

_____

_____

_____

_____

_____

No temptation has overtaken you except what is common to mankind. And God is faithful; he will not let you be tempted beyond what you can bear. But when you are tempted, he will also provide a way out so that you can endure it.

1 CORINTHIANS 10:13

What losses—large or small—have played a part in your
insecurity?

_____

_____

_____

_____

_____

_____

_____

_____

_____

_____

_____

_____

_____

_____

_____

_____

_____

May the LORD answer you when you are in distress;
may the name of the God of Jacob protect you.

PSALM 20:1

In what ways have you experienced rejection in your life? How have these events affected your view of yourself and others?

_____

_____

_____

_____

_____

_____

_____

_____

_____

_____

_____

_____

_____

_____

_____

_____

_____

Jesus and the ones he makes holy have the same Father. That is why Jesus is not ashamed to call them his brothers and sisters.

HEBREWS 2:11, NLT

What changes—good or bad—have produced the most ripples in your life? How have these changes contributed to feelings of insecurity?

_____

_____

_____

_____

_____

_____

_____

_____

_____

_____

_____

_____

_____

_____

_____

_____

_____

_____

_____

Jesus Christ is the same yesterday and today and forever.

Hebrews 13:8

What are some of the limitations you face—physical, mental, financial, relational, etc.? How can you turn these limitations into freedoms?

_____

_____

_____

_____

_____

_____

_____

_____

_____

_____

_____

_____

_____

_____

_____

_____

_____

_____

_____

You will know the truth, and the truth will set you free.

JOHN 8:32

Is there any form of media you need to take a break from? Consider going on a media fast for a period of time, and record what God teaches you through that process.

_____

_____

_____

_____

_____

_____

_____

_____

_____

_____

_____

_____

_____

_____

_____

_____

_____

_____

All glory to God, who is able, through his mighty power at work within us, to accomplish infinitely more than we might ask or think.

EPHESIANS 3:20, NLT

How has pride reared its ugly head in your life? What were the circumstances?

_____

_____

_____

_____

_____

_____

_____

_____

_____

_____

_____

_____

_____

_____

_____

_____

_____

_____

_____

_____

Pride leads to disgrace,
but with humility comes wisdom.

PROVERBS 11:2, NLT

Compare the changelessness of God to the shifting shadows of your own insecurities.

_____

_____

_____

_____

_____

_____

_____

_____

_____

_____

_____

_____

_____

_____

_____

_____

_____

_____

_____

_____

_____

Whatever is good and perfect comes down to us from God our Father,
who created all the lights in the heavens. He never changes or casts
a shifting shadow. He chose to give birth to us by giving us his true
word. And we, out of all creation, became his prized possession.

JAMES 1:17–18, NLT

Read Psalm 121. What strikes you from this passage about the ways God cares for us?

_____

_____

_____

_____

_____

_____

_____

_____

_____

_____

_____

_____

_____

_____

_____

_____

_____

_____

*I lift up my eyes to the mountains—
where does my help come from?
My help comes from the LORD,
the Maker of heaven and earth.*

PSALM 121:1-2

Read Deuteronomy 31:8. How can this verse help you as you deal with loss and rejection?

_____

_____

_____

_____

_____

_____

_____

_____

_____

_____

_____

_____

_____

_____

_____

_____

_____

_____

The LORD himself goes before you and will be with you; he will never leave you nor forsake you. Do not be afraid; do not be discouraged.

DEUTERONOMY 31:8

Read Romans 8:38-39 and then rewrite it in your own words, using examples from your own life.

_____

_____

_____

_____

_____

_____

_____

_____

_____

_____

_____

_____

_____

_____

_____

I am convinced that neither death nor life, neither angels nor demons, neither the present nor the future, nor any powers, neither height nor depth, nor anything else in all creation, will be able to separate us from the love of God that is in Christ Jesus our Lord.

ROMANS 8:38-39

What can you do to make sure your roots are growing deep into Christ?

_____

_____

_____

_____

_____

_____

_____

_____

_____

_____

_____

_____

_____

_____

_____

_____

_____

_____

Let your roots grow down into [Christ], and let your lives be built on him. Then your faith will grow strong in the truth you were taught, and you will overflow with thankfulness.

COLOSSIANS 2:7, NLT

Dear Lord,

You know me better than I know myself. You know why I think like I do and why I feel like I do. You know my every thought. My every disappointment. You know every ugly or ridiculous thing I've ever said or done out of insecurity. You see every fissure in my soul, and You look beyond the point of my failure to the depth of my need. As You reveal Yourself to me, I ask that You also mercifully reveal myself to me. Grant me insight into patterns I've developed, and give me answers that bring healing. Make me wholly unafraid of anything that I might see in myself in the light You provide. Help me to trust that You only shed light where You're willing to heal.

God, You know the complexities of my soul and that most of the time I can't even figure myself out. You know how I swing like a dizzy pendulum between self-loathing and self-exaltation. As I begin this prayer of restoration, I ask You, Lord, to help me take responsibility for the insecurity that is my own doing. My own fault. My own sin. I am painfully aware that I've created some of my own misery. I have tried to make a god of myself too many times, and it hasn't worked. It will never work. In calling me to this time of confession, Your desire is my freedom, not my self-condemnation, so with confidence, I welcome the one and reject the other. With these things in mind, hear my confessions:

_____

_____

_____

_____

_____

_____

_____

_____

_____

_____

_____

_____

_____

_____

_____

_____

_____

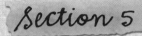

Section 5

She is clothed with strength and dignity;
she can laugh at the days to come.

PROVERBS 31:25

Finding Dignity

This is the very moment we must head straight to the throne of an all-powerful God and Father, rehearsing over and over who He says we are and what He says we're worth. We must call on Him to fight our battles for us and through us and to stand us on steady feet in a confidence only He can supply. We must ask Him to bring forth the women in us we didn't even know we were.

What images or people come to mind when you hear the word *dignity*? Is it something you associate with yourself?

_____

_____

_____

_____

_____

_____

_____

_____

_____

_____

_____

_____

_____

_____

_____

_____

_____

_____

Your beauty should not come from outward adornment, such as elaborate hairstyles and the wearing of gold jewelry or fine clothes. Rather, it should be that of your inner self, the unfading beauty of a gentle and quiet spirit, which is of great worth in God's sight.

1 PETER 3:3-4

What do you think it means to be clothed by God? How could this image help you when you feel weak or find yourself in a vulnerable situation?

_____

_____

_____

_____

_____

_____

_____

_____

_____

_____

_____

_____

_____

_____

_____

_____

_____

_____

Clothe yourselves with the Lord Jesus Christ, and do not think about how to gratify the desires of the flesh.

ROMANS 13:14

How would your life be different if these words described you: *might*, *strength*, and *valor*? What are some specific things that would change?

_____

_____

_____

_____

_____

_____

_____

_____

_____

_____

_____

_____

_____

_____

_____

_____

_____

_____

_____

_____

_____

_____

_____

_____

_____

_____

_____

_____

_____

_____

_____

_____

_____

_____

_____

When I consider your heavens,
the work of your fingers,
the moon and the stars,
which you have set in place,
what is mankind that you are mindful of them,
human beings that you care for them?
You have made them a little lower than the angels
and crowned them with glory and honor.

PSALM 8:3–5

Statements of truth are great weapons against insecurity.
For example:

    God has made me worthy of respect.

    I'm completely clothed by God.

    I am strong in Christ.

What other affirmations might you use in your quest for security?

_____

_____

_____

_____

_____

_____

_____

_____

_____

_____

_____

_____

_____

_____

_____

_____

_____

_____

What shall we say about such wonderful things as these?
If God is for us, who can ever be against us?

ROMANS 8:31, NLT

Read 1 John 5:14-15. What are some things you can ask God for that you know are His will?

_____

_____

_____

_____

_____

_____

_____

_____

_____

_____

_____

_____

_____

_____

_____

_____

This is the confidence we have in approaching God: that
if we ask anything according to his will, he hears us.
And if we know that he hears us—whatever we ask—
we know that we have what we asked of him.

1 JOHN 5:14-15

What would it look like to remain in Christ? What would that feel like?

_____

_____

_____

_____

_____

_____

_____

_____

_____

_____

_____

_____

_____

_____

_____

_____

_____

*If you remain in me and my words remain in you, ask
whatever you wish, and it will be done for you.*

JOHN 15:7

What does genuine humility look like? Are there some areas in your life where you need to let God transform your view of yourself and others?

_____

_____

_____

_____

_____

_____

_____

_____

_____

_____

_____

_____

_____

_____

_____

_____

_____

_____

_____

_____

True humility and fear of the LORD
lead to riches, honor, and long life.

PROVERBS 22:4, NLT

Read Matthew 11:28-30. What are some of the burdens
you are bearing right now? What encouragement does this
passage offer?

_____

_____

_____

_____

_____

_____

_____

_____

_____

_____

_____

_____

_____

_____

_____

_____

_____

*Take my yoke upon you. Let me teach you, because I am humble
and gentle at heart, and you will find rest for your souls. For
my yoke is easy to bear, and the burden I give you is light.*

MATTHEW 11:29-30, NLT

Dear God,

Please forgive me for my self-worship. For my relentless pursuit of control and for my futile attempts at doing Your job. Forgive me for my foolish pride. Forgive me for nursing my ego until it grows so fat that everything touching it bruises it. Forgive me for my miserable self-absorption. Forgive me for the jealousy and covetousness that feed my insecurity. Forgive me for turning too many things into competitions. For being so fixated on what I don't have that I leave the gifts You've given me undeveloped and much less effective than You intended them to be. Forgive me for thinking pitifully little of the person You've made me. Forgive me for committing the flagrant sin of despising myself and considering myself inferior to others. Forgive me equally for every time I've sighed with relief at the thought that I might be superior after all.

Forgive me for my unbelief. If I realized how valuable I am, my insatiable need for affirmation would be quieted. Forgive me for being such a perfectionist that I resist doing something good out of fear that it won't be great. Forgive me for the inordinate self-protection that has only managed to imprison me. Forgive me also for . . .

_____
_____
_____
_____
_____
_____
_____
_____
_____
_____
_____
_____
_____
_____
_____
_____
_____
_____
_____
_____
_____
_____

Section 6

Since we are surrounded by such a great cloud of witnesses, let us throw off everything that hinders and the sin that so easily entangles. And let us run with perseverance the race marked out for us, fixing our eyes on Jesus, the pioneer and perfecter of faith.

Hebrews 12:1-2

Cleared Vision

Jesus is not unhealthy. Not codependent with us. His strength is made perfect in our weakness. This thought never grows old to me: He has no dark side. In Him is *no darkness at all.*

That, beloved, is our challenge. To let the healthy, utterly whole, and completely secure part of us increasingly overtake our earthen vessels until it drives our every emotion, reaction, and relationship. When we allow God's truth to eclipse every false positive and let our eyes spring open to the treasure we *have*, there in His glorious reflection we'll also see the treasure we *are*. And the beauty of the Lord our God will be upon us.

How do you perceive the men in your life? Do you tend to vilify them, or do you put them on a pedestal?

_____

_____

_____

_____

_____

_____

_____

_____

_____

_____

_____

_____

_____

_____

_____

_____

_____

Fear of man will prove to be a snare,
but whoever trusts in the LORD is kept safe.

PROVERBS 29:25

How does your perception of men affect your relationships, your sense of self-worth, and your view of God?

_____

_____

_____

_____

_____

_____

_____

_____

_____

_____

_____

_____

_____

_____

_____

_____

_____

_____

_____

*Hate what is evil; cling to what is good. Be devoted to one
another in love. Honor one another above yourselves.*

ROMANS 12:9-10

Read Galatians 3:26-28. What is most important to our
identities—as men and women alike?

_____

_____

_____

_____

_____

_____

_____

_____

_____

_____

_____

_____

_____

_____

_____

_____

_____

_____

*You are all children of God through faith in Christ Jesus. And all
who have been united with Christ in baptism have put on Christ,
like putting on new clothes. There is no longer Jew or Gentile, slave
or free, male and female. For you are all one in Christ Jesus.*

GALATIANS 3:26-28, NLT

What does it mean to be made in God's image? How does that knowledge affect the way you treat others—male and female?

_____

_____

_____

_____

_____

_____

_____

_____

_____

_____

_____

_____

_____

_____

_____

_____

_____

_____

God created human beings in his own image.
In the image of God he created them;
male and female he created them.

GENESIS 1:27, NLT

How does God want men and women to interact with one
another?

_____

_____

_____

_____

_____

_____

_____

_____

_____

_____

_____

_____

_____

_____

_____

*As a prisoner for the Lord, then, I urge you to live a life worthy
of the calling you have received. Be completely humble and gentle;
be patient, bearing with one another in love. Make every effort
to keep the unity of the Spirit through the bond of peace.*

EPHESIANS 4:1-3

The only way we can develop a healthy, God-honoring view of men is to see them as God sees them. What are some perceptions you need to change to align your view with His?

_____

_____

_____

_____

_____

_____

_____

_____

_____

_____

_____

_____

_____

_____

_____

_____

_____

_____

_____

*The LORD does not look at the things people look at. People look
at the outward appearance, but the LORD looks at the heart.*

1 SAMUEL 16:7

What fears and barriers do you need to overcome in order to take a step of faith toward true security?

_____

_____

_____

_____

_____

_____

_____

_____

_____

_____

_____

_____

_____

_____

_____

_____

_____

When he saw the strong wind and the waves, he was terrified and began to sink. "Save me, Lord!" he shouted.

MATTHEW 14:30, NLT

What steps can you can take to focus on Christ in order to over-come your fears or barriers?

_____

_____

_____

_____

_____

_____

_____

_____

_____

_____

_____

_____

_____

_____

_____

_____

_____

Be strong and courageous, and do the work. Don't be
afraid or discouraged, for the LORD God, my God, is
with you. He will not fail you or forsake you.

1 Chronicles 28:20, NLT

Dear Lord,

Help me to see where I am overly sensitive and where I put too much pressure on relationships. Help me to see where I insist on making a situation all about me. I really want to change. Help me to quit saying, "This is the way I am," and remind me that I am capable of tremendous transformation with You. Deliver me from insecurity in my relationships. Help me to cease being so easily wounded, but at the same time, keep me from growing hardened. Help me to resign my position as a game player and manipulator without resigning myself to a life of misuse. Help me to realize that it's pointless to demand that others love me more or love me better. Real affection cannot be coerced. I cannot put a human in charge of my security without setting him or her up for certain failure. Help me to stop using a person as my mirror and start seeing myself as You alone see me.

Lord, empower me to forgive those who have let me down, failed to protect me, or inflicted injury upon me. Help me to see them as needy, broken people in their own right, and Lord, where there is still life and opportunity, bring redemption to those relationships. Help me to understand the gravity of this juncture: that if I do not seek healing and wholeness, I will instead end up perpetuating the cycle of injury. Break the cycle with me, O Lord. Break the cycle with me.

_____

_____

_____

_____

_____

_____

_____

_____

_____

_____

_____

_____

_____

_____

_____

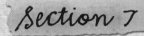

Section 7

I trust in your unfailing love.
I will rejoice because you have rescued me.

PSALM 13:5, NLT

Let God Be God

Trust God.

Plain and simple. Not easy, mind you, but basic and uncompli-
cated. You don't always have to hash it all out. Sometimes you
can make a single swift decision. As Christ said to a wavering
disciple, you just have to make up your splintered mind to "stop
doubting and believe" (John 20:27). Believe that He loves you
and has you covered and takes every one of your hits as if they
were aimed at His own skin. Get down to the bottom of what
frightens you, and then pitch it to Him like a hot potato.

If we can't count on God, for crying out loud, who can we
count on?

Write down the most significant male relationships in your life.
What are some specific ways you want to improve each of those
relationships?

_____

_____

_____

_____

_____

_____

_____

_____

_____

_____

_____

_____

_____

_____

_____

_____

_____

Finish the work, so that your eager willingness
to do it may be matched by your completion of it.

2 Corinthians 8:11

Think of a time you felt threatened by the convictions of a man in your life or a time you were tempted to change a man's convictions. What was behind your fear? How did you respond?

_____

_____

_____

_____

_____

_____

_____

_____

_____

_____

_____

_____

_____

_____

_____

_____

_____

Make every effort to keep yourselves united in the
Spirit, binding yourselves together with peace.

Ephesians 4:3, NLT

Who is it that you most want to control? In what ways does that person (or people) either threaten or strengthen your sense of security?

_____

_____

_____

_____

_____

_____

_____

_____

_____

_____

_____

_____

_____

_____

_____

_____

You must love the LORD your God with all your
heart, all your soul, and all your mind.

MATTHEW 22:37, NLT

What would appropriate authority look like in your situation?
How is that different from excessive control, in both attitude
and actions?

_____

_____

_____

_____

_____

_____

_____

_____

_____

_____

_____

_____

_____

_____

_____

_____

Direct your children onto the right path,
and when they are older, they will not leave it.

PROVERBS 22:6, NLT

How do you know when an attempt to help someone else has turned into a struggle to control him or her? What are some triggers that can tip you off that your desire for control is getting out of hand?

_____

_____

_____

_____

_____

_____

_____

_____

_____

_____

_____

_____

_____

_____

_____

_____

_____

If you try to hang on to your life, you will lose it. But if
you give up your life for my sake, you will save it.

MATTHEW 16:25, NLT

Fill in these blanks: If my loved one would _____,
then I'd be _____. Take some time to release this
person and this situation to God.

_____

_____

_____

_____

_____

_____

_____

_____

_____

_____

_____

_____

_____

_____

_____

_____

_____

_____

_____

*Don't you realize that you become the slave of whatever you
choose to obey? You can be a slave to sin, which leads to death, or
you can choose to obey God, which leads to righteous living.*

ROMANS 6:16, NLT

What changes do you need to leave in God's hands today?

_____

_____

_____

_____

_____

_____

_____

_____

_____

_____

_____

_____

_____

_____

_____

_____

_____

_____

_____

_____

_____

Commit everything you do to the LORD.
Trust him, and he will help you.

PSALM 37:5, NLT

When have you fallen into the trap of thinking you have to know everything—especially about the people closest to you? What are some areas in which it would be healthier for you not to know it all?

_____

_____

_____

_____

_____

_____

_____

_____

_____

_____

_____

_____

_____

_____

_____

_____

_____

_____

_____

You will keep in perfect peace
those whose minds are steadfast,
because they trust in you.

ISAIAH 26:3

Read Psalm 104. Note the wonderful images of God's power that are described in this passage.

_____

_____

_____

_____

_____

_____

_____

_____

_____

_____

_____

_____

_____

_____

_____

_____

_____

_____

_____

Praise the LORD, my soul.
LORD my God, you are very great;
you are clothed with splendor and majesty.

PSALM 104:1

Read Isaiah 55:8-11. What does it mean to you that God's thoughts are higher than yours?

_____

_____

_____

_____

_____

_____

_____

_____

_____

_____

_____

_____

_____

_____

_____

_____

"My thoughts are not your thoughts,
neither are your ways my ways,"
declares the LORD.

ISAIAH 55:8

How does having a more accurate picture of God give you
a better perspective on who you are?

_____

_____

_____

_____

_____

_____

_____

_____

_____

_____

_____

_____

_____

_____

_____

_____

_____

_____

_____

_____

O LORD, our Lord, your majestic name fills the earth!
Your glory is higher than the heavens.

PSALM 8:1, NLT

Read 1 Thessalonians 5:23-24. In what ways is God changing you? What does He promise?

_____

_____

_____

_____

_____

_____

_____

_____

_____

_____

_____

_____

_____

_____

_____

_____

_____

May God himself, the God of peace, sanctify you through and through.

1 THESSALONIANS 5:23

Read Philippians 1:3-6. What are some things you hope God will bring to completion in you? How about in those you love?

_____

_____

_____

_____

_____

_____

_____

_____

_____

_____

_____

_____

_____

_____

_____

_____

_____

_____

_____

He who began a good work in you will carry it on
to completion until the day of Christ Jesus.

PHILIPPIANS 1:6

Dear God,

This very moment I receive Your lavish
forgiveness and Your complete cleansing
and in Your name I release all the
shame that has come from self-inflicted
insecurity. From now on, Lord, and every
day for the rest of my life, heighten my
conviction until I'm instantly aware when
insecurity is my own making. Help me to
recognize any form of pride or unbelief
and to refuse it immediately.

   Now, Lord, I ask You to pull up the roots of
insecurity that were not of my own doing,
and usher in healing and restoration. You
know every single place where instability
has touched my life. You remember details
that were long erased from my memory but
are still inflicting insecurity. You know
what first frightened me into believing that
no one and nothing could be trusted and
that I'm on my own out here in a very
unsafe world. You know the rational origin
of every irrational fear. You know where
I developed a belief system based on the
frailties of man instead of the bedrock of
You. You have been with me every moment,
even when I felt there was no one to take

care of me. I give You my whole heart. Touch every broken and wounded place with Your healing hand.

_____

_____

_____

_____

_____

_____

_____

_____

_____

_____

_____

_____

_____

_____

_____

_____

_____

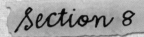

Section 8

Do not throw away your confidence; it will be richly rewarded. You need to persevere so that when you have done the will of God, you will receive what he has promised.

HEBREWS 10:35–36

The Power to Choose

The power to choose is so inherently God given that Scripture raises a gigantic red flag over people who make us feel so weak we can't make a sound decision. A person cannot be whole in a relationship where he or she feels powerless to make healthy choices.

The power to stand at a crossroads and make a good, sound choice based on a solid sense of security is a gift from God straight to the souls of His image bearers. Through His strength, we can choose to speak the truth in love. We can choose life.

What legacy of faith and womanhood have you received from
the women who have gone before you?

_____

_____

_____

_____

_____

_____

_____

_____

_____

_____

_____

_____

_____

_____

_____

_____

_____

*Those who are wise will shine as bright as the sky, and those who
lead many to righteousness will shine like the stars forever.*

DANIEL 12:3, NLT

Can you think of times in your life when your feelings followed your thoughts and actions? Is there a situation you are facing now in which you need to choose what's right, even if your feelings don't match up?

_____

_____

_____

_____

_____

_____

_____

_____

_____

_____

_____

_____

_____

_____

_____

Above all else, guard your heart,
for everything you do flows from it.

PROVERBS 4:23

How do you react to the idea that God gave us emotions and wants us to express them? What are some emotions you've held back from God that you can express to Him now?

_____

_____

_____

_____

_____

_____

_____

_____

_____

_____

_____

_____

_____

_____

_____

_____

_____

Letting your sinful nature control your mind leads to death. But letting the Spirit control your mind leads to life and peace.

ROMANS 8:6, NLT

In what ways do you let others' problems erode your security? How can you combat this tendency?

_____

_____

_____

_____

_____

_____

_____

_____

_____

_____

_____

_____

_____

_____

_____

_____

_____

I am saying this for your benefit, not to place restrictions on you. I want you to do whatever will help you serve the Lord best, with as few distractions as possible.

1 Corinthians 7:35, nlt

What legacy do you want to pass on to the next generation
of women?

_____

_____

_____

_____

_____

_____

_____

_____

_____

_____

_____

_____

_____

_____

_____

_____

_____

_____

_____

_____

We will not hide them from their descendants;
we will tell the next generation
the praiseworthy deeds of the LORD,
his power, and the wonders he has done.

PSALM 78:4

Read Psalm 42. What complaints does the psalmist make? What emotions does he express?

_____

_____

_____

_____

_____

_____

_____

_____

_____

_____

_____

_____

_____

_____

_____

_____

_____

As the deer pants for streams of water,
so my soul pants for you, my God.
My soul thirsts for God, for the living God.

PSALM 42:1-2

Read Deuteronomy 30:19-20. What does it mean to choose life? What would that look like in your life?

_____

_____

_____

_____

_____

_____

_____

_____

_____

_____

_____

_____

_____

_____

This day I call the heavens and the earth as witnesses against you that I have set before you life and death, blessings and curses. Now choose life, so that you and your children may live and that you may love the LORD your God, listen to his voice, and hold fast to him.

DEUTERONOMY 30:19-20

How passionate are you about seeking Christ? What words would you use to describe your pursuit?

_____

_____

_____

_____

_____

_____

_____

_____

_____

_____

_____

_____

_____

_____

_____

_____

_____

_____

_____

_____

_____

_____

_____

_____

_____

_____

_____

_____

_____

_____

_____

_____

_____

_____

_____

_____

Why, my soul, are you downcast?
Why so disturbed within me?
Put your hope in God,
for I will yet praise him,
my Savior and my God.

PSALM 42:11

Ask the Lord for insight about whether there is anything in your close relationships that you need to confront. What boundaries might you need to set?

_____

_____

_____

_____

_____

_____

_____

_____

_____

_____

_____

_____

_____

_____

_____

_____

_____

_____

_____

_____

_____

_____

_____

_____

_____

_____

_____

_____

_____

_____

_____

_____

I waited patiently for the LORD;
he turned to me and heard my cry.
He lifted me out of the slimy pit,
out of the mud and mire;
he set my feet on a rock
and gave me a firm place to stand.
He put a new song in my mouth,
a hymn of praise to our God.
Many will see and fear the LORD
and put their trust in him.

PSALM 40:1-3

Dear God,

Please do not let me confuse healing with betrayal. Help me to see any place in my life where I'm hanging on to my grief or anger in an attempt to hang on to what I've lost. Grant me the gift of healthy grief that does not fight the pain or the process of healing. Lord, please help me to see where I have suffered a substantial loss that I've never regarded. Where I lost innocence, grant me integrity. Where I lost a relationship, grant me true intimacy. Where I lost a home, grant me an internal, unshakable sense of belonging. Where I've held someone responsible for my loss, grant me the ability to forgive. Don't stop until You've made a miracle of me.

_____

_____

_____

_____

_____

_____

_____

_____

Section 9

Your light will break forth like the dawn,
and your healing will quickly appear;
then your righteousness will go before you,
and the glory of the LORD will be your rear guard.
Then you will call, and the LORD will answer;
you will cry for help, and he will say: Here am I.

ISAIAH 58:8-9

Looking beyond Ourselves

If you've suffered a serious case of insecurity, you need to make sure that you're letting God tend to it. Putting up a front doesn't work. That neon light has a way of burning through every cover we throw on it. God knows exactly what happened and what toll it took. He knows the number it played on your mind. Let Him bring you peace. Let Him tell you you're worth *wanting*, *loving*, even *liking*, *pursuing*, *fighting for*, and, yes, beloved, *keeping*.

Whatever you do, don't reject the only One wholly incapable of rejecting you.

What do your closest female friendships mean to you? How do you deal with hurt or insecurity in the context of these relationships?

_____

_____

_____

_____

_____

_____

_____

_____

_____

_____

_____

_____

_____

_____

_____

_____

_____

_____

Where two or three gather together as my followers,
I am there among them.

MATTHEW 18:20, NLT

Has insecurity ever robbed you of what could have been a rich friendship with another woman? Has it affected the type of woman you befriend?

_____

_____

_____

_____

_____

_____

_____

_____

_____

_____

_____

_____

_____

_____

_____

_____

_____

_____

I will give them an undivided heart and put a new
spirit in them; I will remove from them their heart
of stone and give them a heart of flesh.

EZEKIEL 11:19

Have you ever tried to humanize your "rival"? What happened?

_____

_____

_____

_____

_____

_____

_____

_____

_____

_____

_____

_____

_____

_____

_____

_____

_____

Make allowance for each other's faults, and forgive anyone who offends you. Remember, the Lord forgave you, so you must forgive others.

Colossians 3:13, NLT

Think of some examples of secure women you have known.
What have you learned from them?

_____

_____

_____

_____

_____

_____

_____

_____

_____

_____

_____

_____

_____

_____

_____

_____

*These older women must train the younger women to love
their husbands and their children, to live wisely and be pure, to
work in their homes, to do good, and to be submissive to their
husbands. Then they will not bring shame on the word of God.*

TITUS 2:4–5, NLT

How can we encourage other women to find their God-given security?

_____

_____

_____

_____

_____

_____

_____

_____

_____

_____

_____

_____

_____

_____

_____

_____

_____

_____

*Do not think of yourself more highly than you ought, but
rather think of yourself with sober judgment, in accordance
with the faith God has distributed to each of you.*

Romans 12:3

Is there someone in your life who needs your help right now?
How might focusing on another person free you from the self-
absorption of insecurity?

_____

_____

_____

_____

_____

_____

_____

_____

_____

_____

_____

_____

_____

_____

_____

_____

_____

_____

*He makes the whole body fit together perfectly. As each part
does its own special work, it helps the other parts grow, so that
the whole body is healthy and growing and full of love.*

EPHESIANS 4:16, NLT

Do you trust God to redeem the darkest areas of your life for His glory?

_____

_____

_____

_____

_____

_____

_____

_____

_____

_____

_____

_____

_____

_____

_____

_____

_____

In his kindness God called you to share in his eternal
glory by means of Christ Jesus. So after you have suffered
a little while, he will restore, support, and strengthen
you, and he will place you on a firm foundation.

1 PETER 5:10, NLT

Read Galatians 5:22-26. How does celebrating someone else's uniqueness help you overcome jealousy and unhealthy comparisons?

_____
_____
_____
_____
_____
_____
_____
_____
_____
_____
_____
_____
_____
_____
_____
_____

We will not compare ourselves with each other as if one of us were better and another worse. We have far more interesting things to do with our lives. Each of us is an original.

GALATIANS 5:26, *The Message*

What role does the Holy Spirit play in helping you appreciate the good in other people?

_____

_____

_____

_____

_____

_____

_____

_____

_____

_____

_____

_____

_____

_____

_____

What we have received is not the spirit of the world, but the Spirit who is from God, so that we may understand what God has freely given us.

1 CORINTHIANS 2:12

Is there someone in your life you need to love today? What are some specific steps you can take to follow Jesus' command to love that person?

_____

_____

_____

_____

_____

_____

_____

_____

_____

_____

_____

_____

_____

_____

_____

_____

_____

_____

A new command I give you: Love one another. As I have loved you, so you must love one another. By this everyone will know that you are my disciples, if you love one another.

JOHN 13:34-35

The Bible commands us to pray for our enemies. Is there someone in your life who rubs you the wrong way, threatens you, or triggers your insecurity button? Are you willing to pray for that person today? With God's help, consider writing out a prayer.

_____

_____

_____

_____

_____

_____

_____

_____

_____

_____

_____

_____

_____

_____

_____

_____

_____

_____

_____

_____

_____

You have heard that it was said, "Love your neighbor and hate your enemy." But I tell you, love your enemies and pray for those who persecute you, that you may be children of your Father in heaven.

Dear Lord,
Help me to learn how to hang on tight
to You when my life is rocked by dramatic
change. Empower me to trust You and
not to panic or fight for control. Help
me to stop confusing a change in my
circumstances with a change in my security
status. You are my security, O God. You are
the one sure thing. When everything around
me shakes, You are unshakable. Nothing
has the propensity to reveal false gods to me
like a sudden change in my circumstances.
Help me to see them and surrender them
instantaneously. Use change to provoke
what needs changing in me, Lord, and to
increase my appreciation of the only
One who is the same yesterday, today,
and forever.

Section 10

*Trust in the LORD with all your heart
and lean not on your own understanding;
in all your ways submit to him,
and he will make your paths straight.*

PROVERBS 3:5-6

Moving past Fear into Trust

The future we have coming is so glorious that nothing we've suffered will compare to the magnitude and splendor of it. We must not let the enemy of our souls get away with convincing us that anything can utterly destroy us. If we do, we will hand him an engraved invitation to attend our constant torment.

Over and over Jesus implores His followers, "Take courage!" as if His hand is outstretched and His palm opened with offered treasure. It's time we took Him up on it. Do we really want to spend our time rehearsing deaths of all kinds rather than engaging in the effervescence of life?

What circumstances in your life have influenced your ability to trust? How does trusting God differ from trusting other people?

_____
_____
_____
_____
_____
_____
_____
_____
_____
_____
_____
_____
_____
_____
_____
_____
_____
_____
_____
_____

In this world you will have trouble. But take heart!
I have overcome the world.

JOHN 16:33

What do you think it means to really trust God?

_____

_____

_____

_____

_____

_____

_____

_____

_____

_____

_____

_____

_____

_____

_____

_____

_____

_____

You love him even though you have never seen him.
Though you do not see him now, you trust him; and
you rejoice with a glorious, inexpressible joy.

1 PETER 1:8, NLT

If your biggest fears became a reality, who would God be on the other side of such a tragedy?

_____

_____

_____

_____

_____

_____

_____

_____

_____

_____

_____

_____

_____

_____

_____

_____

_____

We know that in all things God works for the good of those who love him, who have been called according to his purpose.

ROMANS 8:28

God promises us eventual good but not painlessness in this life.
How might He bring good out of the pain you're facing now?

_____

_____

_____

_____

_____

_____

_____

_____

_____

_____

_____

_____

_____

_____

_____

_____

_____

The more we suffer for Christ, the more God will
shower us with his comfort through Christ.

2 CORINTHIANS 1:5, NLT

What would your life be like if you were able to "look in triumph" on your enemies? How can you start to do that today?

_____

_____

_____

_____

_____

_____

_____

_____

_____

_____

_____

_____

_____

_____

_____

_____

_____

Their hearts are secure, they will have no fear;
in the end they will look in triumph on their foes.

PSALM 112:8

How would your life change if you stopped asking, "What will I do if . . . ?" and started asking, "What will God do if . . . ?"

_____

_____

_____

_____

_____

_____

_____

_____

_____

_____

_____

_____

_____

_____

_____

_____

_____

They will have no fear of bad news;
their hearts are steadfast, trusting in the LORD.

PSALM 112:7

Which fears do you need God's strength to face today?

_____

_____

_____

_____

_____

_____

_____

_____

_____

_____

_____

_____

_____

_____

_____

_____

_____

_____

_____

_____

_____

_____

_____

The LORD is my light and my salvation—
whom shall I fear?
The LORD is the stronghold of my life—
of whom shall I be afraid?

PSALM 27:1

What is your ultimate desire? What can you do to seek the Lord's face wholeheartedly?

_____

_____

_____

_____

_____

_____

_____

_____

_____

_____

_____

_____

_____

_____

_____

_____

_____

_____

_____

_____

_____

_____

One thing I ask from the LORD,
this only do I seek:
that I may dwell in the house of the LORD
all the days of my life,
to gaze on the beauty of the LORD
and to seek him in his temple. . . .
My heart says of you, "Seek his face!"
Your face, LORD, I will seek.

PSALM 27:4, 8

Are you waiting on the Lord in any area of your life? What gives you strength to hang on?

_____

_____

_____

_____

_____

_____

_____

_____

_____

_____

_____

_____

_____

_____

_____

_____

_____

_____

_____

_____

_____

_____

This vision is for a future time.
It describes the end, and it will be fulfilled.
If it seems slow in coming, wait patiently,
for it will surely take place.
It will not be delayed.

<small>HABAKKUK 2:3, NLT</small>

What do you find most comforting about God's presence
in your life?

_____

_____

_____

_____

_____

_____

_____

_____

_____

_____

_____

_____

_____

_____

_____

_____

_____

_____

_____

_____

_____

God is our refuge and strength,
an ever-present help in trouble.
Therefore we will not fear, though the earth give way
and the mountains fall into the heart of the sea,
though its waters roar and foam
and the mountains quake with their surging.

PSALM 46:1-3

What has God done in your life through this journey toward
soul-deep security? Where would you like to go from here?

_____

_____

_____

_____

_____

_____

_____

_____

_____

_____

_____

_____

_____

_____

_____

_____

_____

In that day he will be your sure foundation,
providing a rich store of salvation, wisdom, and knowledge.
The fear of the LORD will be your treasure.

ISAIAH 33:6, NLT

Dear God,
I thank You for all You have done to get
me to this place and for the plan You
have ahead for me. I come now, Lord, to
the apex of my petition: please restore
to my soul all that insecurity has stolen
from me. Overturn every single thing the
enemy meant for evil into something good.
Perform a miracle on me, Lord. Cover me
with Your trustworthy hand. Clothe me
with strength and dignity. Transform what
drives me. Quell what triggers me. Make me
a courageous woman in this harrowing
culture. One who refuses to be reduced and
defined by the media. Help me to make
conscious decisions about whether or not the
cost of what they're selling is worth buying.
Give me the discernment to call a lie a lie.

   Make me the kind of woman a little girl
could follow to dignity and security. I
actively and deliberately receive—and
vow to keep receiving—everything that
I have requested in Your will this day.
Let this statement reverberate into every

corner of my life and invade the bone marrow of my belief system: Today on _____ [date], I receive my dignity back. No one and nothing can take it from me because You are the One who gave it. Help me to recognize that I've lost my dignity only because I have surrendered it. Empower me to claim it back and hang on to it with all my might. Because of Your mercy, Lord, I am no fool. Only a wise woman shifts her trust to You.

In Jesus' saving and delivering name, Amen.

_____
_____
_____
_____
_____
_____
_____
_____
_____
_____
_____

My Father in heaven,
I thank You for breath this day to give You praise.
   I thank You for a life where nothing is wasted,
   a life where pain turns into purpose and Your providence assigns a personal destiny.
   You will never allow anything in my path
   that cannot bring You glory or me and those around me good.
   No matter what this day holds,
   I am clothed with strength and dignity.
   I have divine strength to overcome every obstacle and all oppression
   because I belong to Jesus Christ, and His Spirit lives within me.
   You, Lord, are my security.
   No one and nothing can take You from me.
   You will keep my foot from being caught in a trap.
   I choose to turn my back on fear because You are right here with me.
   I can smile over the days to come because Your plan for me is good and right.
   My heart is steadfast, trusting in You, Lord.

In the end, I will look in triumph on my foes.
Because of You,
I, _____, am secure.
In Jesus' triumphant name,
Amen.